MW00592695

LOVE-IN-IDLENESS

Poems by

Christopher Hennessy

Brooklyn Arts Press ·New York

LOVE-IN-IDLENESS
© 2011 Christopher Hennessy

ISBN-13: 978-1-936767-02-1

Published in The United States of America by:
Brooklyn Arts Press
154 N 9th St #1
Brooklyn, NY 11211
WWW.BROOKLYNARTSPRESS.COM
INFO@BROOKLYNARTSPRESS.COM

Distributed to the trade by Small Press Distribution / SPD.
www.spdbooks.org

Library of Congress Control Number: 2011930911

"Rosanna" © 1982 CBS, Inc. From Toto's album *Toto IV*.

Cover Art and Design by David Drummond. Photograph
of Christopher Hennessy by Rhea Becker.

FIRST EDITION

ACKNOWLEDGMENTS

To Anthony, with all my love. And for my parents, for all their love and support.

Sincerest thanks to Eric Schramm for his friendship, love, poems and guidance over the years. Thanks to both Eric and R.J. Gibson for help in preparing these poems for the world. Thanks to John Skoyles for mentoring—and believing in—a young man who needed the permission to speak about desire and difference and the craft to turn that speech into poetry. And lastly, I owe a huge debt of gratitude to Joe Millar at Brooklyn Arts Press for his superlative editorial insight and his unswerving dedication to making this book tell the story it was meant to tell. The author would also like to dedicate many of the poems in the first section to the memory of his grandparents R. and M. Koch and R. and B. Hennessy.

Thanks to the editors of these journals for publishing the following poems, sometimes in earlier versions: "A Split Secret," *Ploughshares*; "Autopsy," *OCHO*; "After My Grandmother's Funeral," *Court Green*; "Christopher Looks," *Night Train*; "The Cicada, and Other Lessons" (as "The Cicada Lessons"), *Knockout*; "Gethsemane," *Memorious*; "'I Hand You Like an Orange to a Child.'" *Anti-*; "Icarus on the Moon," *Touchstone*; "Love-in-Idleness" (as "A Glut of Fallen Leaves"), *Wisconsin Review*; "Love Poem to Carl Linnaeus," *Court Green*; "The Lover's Story," *Natural Bridge*; "Mud, Milk, Snow, Mud" (as "Terra Firma"), *Cimarron Review*; "Nocturne," *Court Green*; "Nietzsche, Pasolini & I," *Memorious*; "Jacob (as "The Seduction of Jacob"), *Natural Bridge*; "Pear, Apple, Peach," *Crab Orchard Review*; "Sick Room," *Bloom*; "Still Life with Jars," *Brooklyn Review*; "Thief," *Knockout*; "Waiting Room," *Full Circle Journal*; "Wreckage," *Cimarron Review*, "'You are the pin-holder,'" *Wisconsin Review*.

"Icarus on the Moon" and "Epithalamion" also appeared in *This New Breed: Gents, Bad Boys and Barbarians 2*, edited by Rudy Kikel. "Carriers" will appear in the anthology *A Face to Meet the Faces: An Anthology of Contemporary Persona Poetry*, edited by Stacey Lynn Brown and Oliver de la Paz.

CONTENTS

ALMOST A BEDROOM

CHRISTOPHER LOOKS

Christopher looks like he's been spit out,
like a too-salty piece of meat,
like an unwanted thought.

Like a mannequin, a man made of teak,
a talking prune.

Christopher looks like I'm having trouble creating him,
or like he could be the father of purpose.

Christopher looks like a turtle negotiating
a path of slick stones. If you don't know
what Christopher looks like, visualize
a garden gnome in crisis.

Some days Christopher looks like an ordinary young man;
others, like a man dying to get out alive, gone
into his dead man's suit at the first sight of blood.

Christopher looks like someone you will recognize
if you go to heaven. Christopher looks like he's in hell
as he stammers through an apology for not calling.

Christopher looks like a frightened scarecrow,
like a little boy wrapped in a bumblebee bowtie.
Like he's trying and failing
to strangle himself with his black cravat.

Christopher looks like your trunk is full of bodies.

THE CICADA, AND
OTHER LESSONS

IF RECRIMINATIONS

1

Do you think that if Rosey B. had noticed
your song request—Toto's "Rosanna"—
that you could have made out your future
in the punch bowl's quavering ruby ripples?

Rosanna, Rosanna, I didn't know you
were looking for more than I could ever be.

2

Do you think, had the world
been bigger than a country block, and you
more (or less) aged than the Cass River's mud-
aged carp, if the seasons hadn't overtaken
the local news and rumors and lawn care,

3

that you would have made that promise to yourself
in a place named Pigeon, Michigan, amid quiet
snowfall, the smell of diesel and sweat rising
like a team of horses stamping at the frosted black
as you walked to the yellow bus, sucking in
the cold-as-metal air?

4

Do you think that if you hadn't hidden
in plain sight on the playground, the boys
on the blacktop who doffed their shirts
at recess (hot brown backs in the sun)

would have let you in on their dirty joke,
taught your armpit how to fart, or later demanded
out behind the bus garage that you 'touch it'?

5

Do you think B.J. would see your body
tense, then vibrate (attuned to shame)
as Duckie sissed, *This is a really volcanic ensemble*
you're wearing, it's really marvelous—B.J. in his underwear,
you—Jesus!—still in PJs, tipping your cup of Faygo
Redpop onto the carpet like a sudden bleed?

6

Do you think that if a summer storm
thundered in from nowhere, stranding you
in the little red barn where Dad keeps his
musky bags of mulch, where the rain soaks
a neighbor boy's t-shirt through, every curve
slicked and sticking skin to fabric,
you could still find space for a breath,
find and hold tight the dark seconds
breaking angrily across the sky?

YELLOW

for my sister

The boy who smokes walks the aisle of the bus
whacking the cotton hats off the runts' heads.
When he sees you, he calls out *Lisa, pizza,*
pepperoni pizza! Chinese, Chinese, where they all eat doggies.

    That was the day we learned about Alaska and the Inuit.
    The whale blubber, the dog sleds, the snow shoes.
    The ice floes adrift with old women on them.

Your cheek is like the thumb-bruised
petal of a slighted flower. Eyes black
as the anise candies we get after supper.
Tonight I steal a fork, hide it in my bag.
Tomorrow, calm in class, I'll pluck its tines.

THE BLESSING

Neither of us knew,
but I was as cruel as his April
ritual of trapping toads, crawdads,
snapping turtles, easy quarry, then
duct taping each alive and wriggling
to M-83, the highway sucked clean
and black by sheets of white rain.

Neither of us knew, being criminals,
why this arcane fetish, why the want
of squash and the taste for gush
of what's inside, turned out.

Could it be it was too simple
to refuse to turn away from
his lean torso as passing cars
ripped apart his helpless targets?

What followed was a blessing,
watching as he dipped his naked body
into the deep, rain-filled ditch—white
underwear hanging like a torn flag
from the broken, hung limb of an oak.

AUTOPSY

My slippery virgin heart is ripe,
ta-tumming in the circular gape
I carve. Up to elbow in tripe,

I grip my guts' tentacles, bare-
handed, wrestle them from a mire
of the living, wavy hairs

that stick to my sides. In tears, I plumb
deeper, desperate to thumb
out the bleating organ (goddamn

ta-tumming), set it on a platter
surrounded by the seeds of cancer,
a burlesque of eggs, boiled and bitter.

As white as the worm
that eats through my sternum,
how empty the body's become.

How hollowed by flame.
A flicker worshiped lights the shame.
Hallowed be your name.

There is no heart in a pumpkin-
shaped boy who eats out his in-
sides to suck on his sin.

NOCTURNE

I would be found laying in the dark
in the smooth basin of an empty tub
like a fish frozen, my eyes open,
my blue pajamas washed in piss.

Mother said I'd mutter what sounded
like numbers in some other language,
the sound *like heavy breathing, a lost boy*
running up a long, long flight of stairs.

But I was cataloguing another life: alien
beings, superheroes, secret agents,
the boys in school I wanted
to be but couldn't even talk to.

Dawn brought white wake-
fulness, a mumble of some lucid self,
light like a suture through my lips.
Only at night did the gland of my mind
wink open, a black iris in mid-eclipse.

MUD, MILK, SNOW, MUD

Wandering in circles in the dark
silo, I was the final grandson
to see the farm begin

its dying, a slow plodding
led by the two wolfish guards of the hencoop,
Keiko and Smoky. Big enough to ride,

but with broken sloped backs, they slouched,
sore beasts of burden, stuck in a muddy hole
clawed out from the clay surrounding

their shingled kennels. I dug into matted hides,
held as they shook me, and a musk rose up—
part loam, part rot—that burned as I breathed it in.

Smoky, a mother then, though no one knew,
began to shiver, a rumble caught in her lungs.
And from deep in the barn, with rafters like ribs

of a great carcass, a slow snap of bones echoed.
And the word *hobble* bubbled up from grandpa's throat
as he emerged from that skeletal coffer, heaving.

    ***

With a hose, we slowly filled
the cow's water trough—big enough
for a child to hide in.

I wanted to swing myself up
and over, splash into the clear,
drinkably cool water, let the cows

lap at me, nudge me, like a calf,
out of the way. I wanted the hose
turned on me, to soak me so wet

I would prune up, turn old
in an instant and know everything
about every animal—how milk is thickened,

how the egg is shaped, why children
don't come back, the muddy
gurgles of birth,

why rabbits are silent creatures
until guileless teeth pull them apart.
And why does the cow rustle

deeper into the hay, its eyes
open, as if expecting a blow
from above?

    ***

Two boys squirreling through the haymow,
we toss dry strands of hay and clap

at a summer snow we make
with this food, this bed. Below us
a row of sad cows chew and nod.

We must find the creaking boards
beneath the itch of our bare feet.
So much hay to scoop,

we drown in dust. Each clap or stomp
dislodges a puff of chaff
from your damp, blonde rooster tail.

***

The farm was unraveling,
each of my three living aunts
invisibly worrying the thread of their mother

as she stood over the one well, biting
her worn lip, cranking a black ink
of water up from a pit stabbing

so deep into the earth it passes hell.
Little watery souls, I imagined, must hide
in her bucket—children lost

to young mothers.
How else explain her grief?
Those hard stones of sweat,

and thickening veins crowning
the scalp? Overcome, she bends,
the tin pail a scale's weight

tilting her into a fractured curtsy.
The bucket tips, dust
becomes mud, and she falls against

the altar of the well,
calling for her children,
each name a star.

GROSS ANATOMY OF THE MIDWESTERN BODY

Cranium

Aunt Bert shuffles around the sun
porch in a pink and yellow apron
that reaches to her duck feet.
She is the smallest in a set
of Russian nesting dolls.
Her unattended stare.
Her hands resting in her lap.
A mind tethered to a horse's kick.

Facies

Which uncle's carbuncular face
is a blistered wound?
They all look the same
after the steam and press
of forty years under the metal thumbs
of the merciless line.

Oculus

Father's once hooked-out eye—
from a boy's thumb
as he ran a lay-up
—is now crooked
and half-curtained,
the lid left to die.

Lingua

My tongue is a flimsy ribbon,
too wide and unrolling past
my lips. It is a dazed worm,
confused by the simplest
desires. It sputters out
lisped pleas, like *Stay back.*
Come close.

Columna vertebralis

Grandma's spine
is rent into a question
by years of carrying two
heavy pails of cancer's milk.

Antebrachium

Great-Grandpa pins the empty
shirtsleeve (where the elbow
should be) into tight little squares.
The day his son was born
he left his arm—forgotten
in the haste for home—
somewhere in the far field,
torn off and sown with the corn.
When the pin pricks him, he smiles.

Phalanges

Grandpa has a red-black fang
that hangs off his swollen finger,
snagging where a nail would scratch.

Manus

Brother's five fingers
hide, a sleeping fist, in the fresh
pulp of sawdust at our feet.
We bury them under a stone.

Membrum inferius

Great-Grandma had
a wooden peg for a leg,
after the bite of a long nail
left a spidery trail of rot.
She finished the shed
before the peg was fit.

Corpus

There is always a body
that never had a chance
to earn its scars.
We give them names,
at least, and bury them—
Tiny Blue Cousin.

ANAPHORA

Carry me away to where the hen house
is row after row of sleepy eyes that bite deep
into the chromosomes, our fungible blood.

Carry me back to you, like the brown egg
cupped in your girl-child's hand. Slip on
the rotten corn husks spilling from the silo

and your palms will close, will break me
open. Carry me back to the morning cry of the sun's
immaculate agony, when I broke you open.

Carry me anyway! Past the vines jeweled
purple with grapes, the spigot, the dinner bell,
the bedbugs warming the attic. Carry me

to bed—where a young mother's vagina
swells like a great, giving eye;

where a wishbone dries on the windowsill,
a chalk beginning to crust its joint;

where the miotic feint of a mitosis lost
deep inside anneals me to your love, this history.

AFTER MY GRANDMOTHER'S FUNERAL

for my mother

A blizzard is roaring outside the kitchen window,
making the birches out back a flock of shivering
black eyes.   Why is it so hard for me to place

a hand on your shoulder
as you shudder, not for her, but for each death,
and the nothing that waits?   The men

of our family say the women of our family are granite-
willed farm girls, the ice of Michigan winters shimmering
under calloused skin.   To hell with them, with the will-

full blindness of men. You hated a man once, only once: fat Mr. Cobb,
the grocer who bought eight seasons of your 4H rams.

You remember every ram's name   (the ewes' have faded):
twins Frank and Hank, black-booted Sam, your first, Buck Owens.
So many, and each so pretty,   blue ribbons through their ears.

"YOU ARE THE PIN-HOLDER,"

mother says as she hangs angels
on the line to dry.

I am the pin-holder,
the baby son naked to the waist.

The railroad-tie posts shudder
as if their train has found them.

With dusk, the heat lightning flashes,
and from past the craters the breeze

brings the smell of the Great Lake
that's shrunk under the sun.

My stunted arms stick
to the sides of my puffy stomach.

And the little glories tug at their pins,
spasm—a flurry of white skins.

Mother whistles. A seraph blinks,
half-asleep, and makes a leafy cough.

Father returns. Slops a string of pike
at mother's feet: *clean these, and cook them.*

He plucks an angel from the line,
wipes his face and limps into the house.

Mother bows her head, fixes on
the wound of grime given to the ghost

that now rests in her hand,
little lace fringes tickling her wrists.

THE KISS

Of course I feared them.
Who wouldn't? Honeycomb
like a cortex of coral,
the black-ribbed cap on sick

whitish stalks poking obscenely
from the dirt. Their cousins
can kill: a genetic blood bond,
code enough for me.

Even when mother fried them,
the little brains dancing
on skates of melting butter,
they looked more animal than plant

—soft flesh, an organ of edible rot.
Father, you called them 'miracles',
would inhale the scent. *Like a rain-
wet faun slept here*, you once said.

*Remember, the dying elms
make morels thrive*—a whisper,
as you held my girlish wrist
and dragged me shivering

through the dark trails of long-
forgotten orchards, past
the wood's mossy trunks
of ash and yellow poplar.

That they ate death, their wetness
a curse, I could forgive. But you
plucked one from its dead
sleep and ate it on the spot.

You made me watch you swallow
the soft cap whole, and I knew you
saw I wouldn't have my own, that I
feared its kiss as much as I missed yours.

TO MY FATHER'S BLUE TUXEDO

The winter I turn 17 I find you hiding
in the back of his closet, wilting
on your hanger. Rumpled, crinkled,

dusted with age's mothwing fuzz.
Your blue is powder-soft,
with baby-blue trim and lapels ruffled,

but you slump, hang limp like a faggot
has just fled you, like he will at his prom,
eager for a jerk-off to a tableau of tuxedoed jocks.

You won't recall, but I saw you once before
in a photo, posing on the body of a man
who looked like me, his hair so wet with sweat

bits of rice stuck in it. His face flush
with June sun, cheap champagne—
simple abundance and simple poverty.

Outside ice hangs on trees. Limbs
snapping like balls smacking
open hands in an end zone.

Winter will never marry us: the fag
sick with threat, the ex-quarterback slamming
a meaty fist into his reddening palm.

GHOST BOY

for my father

You say wild dogs wailed and snarled
each time the Crick sisters left home
to skulk about the market for salt
and butter sticks, all they could afford
to sauté what folks assumed they hunted for
in woods where dogs wouldn't go—
slick morels and stalks of asparagus.

One squat and wrinkled, the other rickety in height,
they smoked black pipes that clicked against their teeth.
No one knew why they impaled the ancient hickory
standing guard out front with dozens of rusted ten-penny spikes,
driven so poorly they arced like the fingernails of crones.

You whisper when you recount the oneiric night
you crept along the house's edge as a kid,
peeking through the grime-caulked windows,
hoping for proof they were witches, or worse.

But always you stop the story there. What did you see?
I'm left imagining a grim-faced child pressing the ghost
of his palms against the glass, a boy who sees the rumor
of his future in the black glass. No old hands will hold him.
No deviance mothers him down. This house is no cage, but a life.

WRECKAGE

A man's three children and slippered wife
watch him from the kitchen window.
He stands a shovel on its head, lights his pipe.
The snow builds layers on his shoulders.
He might need to bury the dog,
but more likely, he's out in the cold
just to smoke, the pipe's thick liquor scent
number one on the list of faults

that makes his wife throw her hands
in the air, without a word; the children
huddle together, hold to her skirt, and wait
for the snow to die down, to glimpse
the wreckage of their father's Michigan winter,
a day he should have spent inside.
Through the snow's scrim they catch him
wedging suet in the crook of a sapling birch,

watch him as he watches a sparrow fret away
at the suet, picking fatty scabs from the belly.
The birds survive the winter like this.
See him slouched next to the white tree? He breaks
into the bark of ice covering the ground
for no reason, his spade now wedged there.
He looks back to see his family watching him,
wondering why he's out in this weather,

which task is so heavy on his shoulders
he's got to finish it today. Five below. The wind
kicks up. The sparrow leaves. Suet wobbles
in its crook, looks as if it will dislodge. The father
puffs his pipe, his teeth clacking on the black stem.
No one knows what to do next.
If they've even a choice in the matter.
Winter sounds a crack along the tree's spine.

LOVE-IN-IDLENESS

A glut of leaves clogs the gutters
so the weight of their mass death
blackens, softens to an ooze.
Father will force me
to scoop the trenches clean
with my bare hands.

He taps his foot on our roof's
chalky shingles, barks out my name,
waits, swats at the fingers
of autumn's skeletal branches.
His swaying trees betray him,
a distraction to hide me, his pansy

son lisping a prayer caught in the clot
of vines and shrubs that edge the house.
I can hear the trough's ooze move,
a writhing, like the mole I found
drowning in the backyard pool,
a wadded hairshirt, convulsing—

it was my job to wade in, pluck it out
and fling it to the blind woods
where the dogs are buried.
With so much rendered inevitable,
how could a boy, surrounded,
do anything but dread the living?

As he parts the branches
to search the bloated gray sky,
a prayerfulness overtakes him.
The grit of his teeth loosens,
and he points to a storm cloud
rolling patiently toward us.

THE CICADA, AND OTHER LESSONS

Hook out the eye
of a fish you've caught
and use it for a lure
if the minnows
and worms are gone
and the tin pail is empty.

Fry the fish with salted butter
and Old Mother Hubbard.
Till the guts into the garden
to grow more squash.

Value each trick a body offers.

***

Identify the killdeer by its call
as it ranges over the mudflats.

Hear the katydids argue
amongst themselves,
pretending to be leaves.

Johnny jump up, heartsease, call-me-
to-you, love-in-idleness…
memorize these names
given to *Viola tricolor*, the pansy.

But know that knowing what to call a thing—
to understand the need its song speaks—

doesn't let you love it, doesn't give you
the right to make it love you back.

***

The cicada sleeps
underground for 17 years
to avoid the mantis and wasp.
But when it emerges, it sings.

There is no shame in that life.

SPLIT SECRETS

CARRIERS

The filament in my throat rattles,
a burnt-out bulb in a shaking fist.
At least the hollowing sound has replaced
the electric hum of my asthma.
And my wings, how sore, pressed
deep into my spine. Each feather
feels like the wooden leaf
of a great desk I carry on my back.

At my age, I dread each sortie.
He lays on us two leaden words
instead of the usual one—
Take care. They easily flake
into pieces of brittle slate
if you hold them too tight.
I have little hands and must hug
the words precious to my chest,
keep my wings in check.

Don't tell a soul, but once,
over the Azure Coast, I felt a letter
slipping from me. In panic,
I dropped the whole word.
Forgive me, I was distracted—
a naked young man was singing hymns,
his long fingers separating tangled
grape vines. He heard the rattle
in my lungs, or noticed
the shadow I laid across his chest
when I flew overhead, the sweat
suddenly cool on his skin.

He looked up, and the word
I'd let slip slid easily
down his throat....
My ecstasy was in imagining
what it must feel like to swallow
a word fallen from the sky.
I hope it was a nice, rich noun.
Peach, or *maelstrom*.

THIEF

They find me hugging myself, knees
to chest, and I remember I chose to hide,
to freeze, staring at a stolen avocado.
Not since that death have I looked up.

I can taste the talc of the empty mouth
I tried to close—I wouldn't eat the fruit;
the ache of feeding on the wind
was punishment for admitting hunger.

I see the rotten pads of my feet,
the bony eruptions in ankle and thigh,
the skin of my knees split.
They say I'm a *complete* find,

but my face has been polished away
like a sand statue, eyes melted
into my head, paper throat collapsed,
necklace beads swallowed by skin.

Even lost, I feared discovery
and the creeping numbness, watching
feathers of ice silt my long black hair,
a fever's sweat crusting into snow on my skin,

my lungs bruising with each breath.
The whole sky thrummed as if plunging
toward me, the terror ripping my mouth
open at the corners...

        What I would give to be
again full of will and hunger—

to plumb the well of my gut
for the wind I'd swallowed,

to give it back to its god. Redeemed,
I would hold a heart, even mine,
beating—a hot, slippery fruit.
I could call out for completion.

QUEEN

A huge, spangled red wig hides
the spindles of Gloriana's thinning hair
as she feasts on sweets all day.
Teeth black and rotten, and still

you think her beautiful,
still keep your sex to yourself
and skulk around the house, fearing
that an army of muscled Norfolks,

freshly fed from the gym,
usurpers all, plot her rape.
"Be my Little Walsingham?"
you ask—and then send me to Spain.

***

You'd have me supper
on her favorite flower.
You call it *heartsease*
or sometimes, feeling pale,
yellow and as anemic
as the word *pansy*,
use the name *love-
in-idleness*.

Our house bursts with them.
Purple, blue and bronze,
pink, lavender and white,
apricot and orange. They leave
a scent like the cologne
of another man in our bed.

***

Her favorite dance is lavolta,
the scandal of the man grasping
his partner's waist, thrusting
him high above his head.

We never dance. In bed
all day, your arm rests dead
against my back.

***

Should I take on the sick dourness
of her flour-chalk mask?
You no longer caress my face,
trace the rough edge of beard only

to powder over the neglect,
reciting the morning recipe:
eggs, shells powdered,
well water, poppy seeds,
borax, alum.

You apply the threat
with your fingertips—white
laced with invisible toxins.

***

"They had to saw the Coronation
Ring off her finger, her flesh
had grown so tightly around
its gold…"

ROSALINE

O brawling love!
he said, ripe
to be choked—
his so-called 'love'
for me a clumsy
jerk-off fantasy.

O loving hate!
he said, and I admit
I thought about
the childish pout,
the serpentine lisp
of his bawling poems,
the loamy odor
of his armpits.

…the all-seeing sun
Ne'er saw his match since first the world begun.
he proclaimed of me—
not her, my red-lipped
cousin, the thin one,
the wanted one.
But I was his first!

Feather of lead, bright smoke, cold fire, sick health!
But I pushed him
off me, as off a cliff.
And in his fall, so unfair,
I became his shadow, a scrim
which blanked the promise
of a second kiss.

THE LOVER'S STORY

Emperor Ai of the Han Dynasty, rather than wake his lover,
asleep on his royal gown, cut the sleeve as proof of his devotion.

To trace my name onto his back
was enough to make him want me.
I needed only a push to the ground,
the choke of his panicked kiss.

Sleepily, I circled him, entranced,
then a languorous fall
to his feet to trail my tongue
ankle to waist,

the seduction concealed
under the robe. Blindness,
the perfect muscle of faith.
Imagining ourselves strangers.

After sex, I only pretended to sleep,
nesting in the folds of his robe.
Hidden in the sleeve—a purple sail.
I chewed my lip to keep awake,

fearing I might admit to a trust
in his love or a promise of mine.
Had I heard the rip as his teeth cut
into the robe's silk, I'd have shouted:

Old Fool, you ruin your gown
for a delicate coward, for the hush
of your mouth on mine.
Or, had we not been so in love,

I could have whispered:
My emperor, make soft noises
as you leave, quick gasps of grief,
so I can hold myself to the dark.

ICARUS ON THE MOON

The day's moon winks in and out of sight
as I pursue it through the clouds.
It is still at a distance, but why save my strength
for a safe landing? I never planned on going home.

Father calls me back, frantic I will ruin
his waxy masterpiece; little does he know
that once I punch past the gauzy airless layers
I will slough off his gadgety sticks, these flaps and feathers.

I've perfected my own machine, deep in my head,
with toothed-wheels pressing a flimsy brain
into cog-shaped will, all powered by thoughts
of hairless moon men with skin like egg shells.

He'll tell Mother how he tried to save me—
old, milk-eyed jealousy having him mistake
a pair of wings for recklessness.
He'll say he skimmed the waters for hours.

Will tell his friends what a good son I would
have made (after a bit of hammering and tinkering),
yet able only to remember the time he caught me
fucking one of the pubescent bull slayers?

On the moon I'll have breath enough
for a life of lovers at all hours; I'll be seizing
ecstasy, a flying wild man—no one's son.
No gravity. Only libido, my breath causing

new eddies of atmosphere. The moon—so close—
like all things desired, more or less there.

A SPLIT SECRET

the story of St. Sebastian's lover

i.

Our shredded tunics a rope,
I tethered his naked stem of a body

to the dogwood we'd chosen:
thready, leafless branches,

a moon-polished bark
burnished. Like his skin

the day he stepped from the river
onto a slate ledge where he lay

naked, bronzed by the sun.
I watched him watch me

and for the first time
I had no secrets to tell.

Later, he let me brush the sand
from his stomach and chest.

Just a boy, when he yawned
the bones in his hips showed.

I tied the tethers too loose,
but he pulled himself tight

while we waited, the skin taut
over his stomach, those hips.

ii.

Caesar's loyal archers were close.
Shaking, I blessed the arrow

I would send to his heart:
the first shot a prayer

for an instant, perfect death.
But I could neither hear nor see,

the buzz of last night's sex
still trilling in my brain.

I began to reel, to slip;
he bowed his head—

for us, a secret gesture:
take my face in your hands.

I tasted a slick of sweat
everywhere I kissed,

like that day at the river,
his damp, coiled ringlets.

iii.

I was knotting his blindfold
when the archers arrived.

Twenty men.
Each with five arrows.

Stretching toes to the ground,
Sebastian traced circles in the dirt.

The Spirit descended—
a clot in my throat,

arms rigid, eyes clear.
Sebastian bowed his head.

I walked to the line.
I couldn't see his eyes.

iv.

After, an archer sighed and softly
thumbed Sebastian's eyes shut, saying:

Caesar was right. He's so beautiful.
And just a boy.

Even now? Even branched
with arrows, skin bleached

but with a constellation
of red puncture ticks?

Yet so little blood.
No, Caesar was wrong.

And martyr is an ugly word—
a split secret, a coward's thumb.

JACOB

To recall your celibate poise
could be my life's work, so blinded

by seeing you on your back,
lying on tucked wings to cushion

my rigid, artless fucking.
A luster of sweat has licked you

blue as a flame, a seamless sheen;
your spine is the verge of heaven,

muscles iced by pleasure. Only the quiver
of your pout saved me from pitying you.

The shock was finding human curves:
collarbone, hips, lean thighs,

the breastbone's aching well.
My guilt is my still wanting you—

an obscene failure of will.
In the shudder of bones,

in the animal spit of ejaculate,
I want you, would again wrestle you

to the ground and deny prophecy
if only to name your beauty.

GETHSEMANE

May this cup be taken from me.

I can rest here, deserted
by the only men who love me,

the freight of grief I carry for them
left to uncurl in the sun like a dying

stem in my palm. I kneel
among the tendrils to study

the stand I will take to prove my guilt.
For a moment, I deny I was begotten,

not created—the life-line on my hand,
a wrinkled, imperfect proof.

I've always known my true life would begin
and end in a garden like this, my will not free,

my breath not Word, everything in bloom—
but the bloom the wound of a pupil

overtaking the eye. A dark comfort.
Because my errant whisper, even muted

by a wall of leaves, becomes prophecy,
I've never said what I feel:

that I would die to live
as a carpenter's son, to see

my rough hands make a thing
as real and inhuman as I am;

that I dream of being only a thing,
a wooden box filled with flowers

set next to an untended grave.
How I would cherish my part

in the bread of such an act,
in the artful life of holding the dead.

"I HAND YOU LIKE AN ORANGE TO A CHILD."

Subject to breaking up
are all compounded things.

With mindfulness
strive on.

—The Buddha's final words

I

I can't sleep.
Fetch me coffee: I'm going to write.
  Mehr Licht!
  Turn up the lights—
(I don't want to go home in the dark).
Read some more.
That tastes good.
  That's good.

II

Little Cousins,
I must go in, the fog is rising.
Now day and night are locked in combat.
The Earth is suffocating.
Do you hear the rain? Do you?
Hear the rain?

It is walking towards me, without hurrying.
Everything is mortal.
I see black light. I am content.

III

Pardonnez-moi, monsieur.

(I don't think they even heard me.)

Pardonnez-moi, monsieur.

(I don't think they even heard me.)
(I don't think they even heard me.)
(I don't think they even heard me.)

Adieu mes amis. Je vais à la gloire!

IV

Das ist absurd! We must be on you,
                        but cannot see you.

Only one man ever understood me.
(μή μου τους κύκλους τάραττε.)
And he really didn't understand me.

V

The paper
burns, but the words

fly free.

O, holy
simplicity.

I am in flames

THE ESTRANGEMENT

After Wayne Koestenbaum's essay "The Poetics of Indifference"

It seemed truly moved that I lifted my head to watch it enter the room, really nothing more than an uncluttered space. But then it seemed to think I couldn't care less. "You didn't care a damn anyway," it said. "Gradually, I cared to wonder about you less and less," I admitted. It had become like a patient who waited for a doctor, but who secretly wondered, *Will I ever be seen? Will I ever leave this musty antechamber?*

The light, if any, appears. Dim epiphany? Would it scour the carnal operation of our tediums, our noises? The grunts, if any, are low. Sex is a homoerotic lemon. When my hand or voice goes lax, unsupple, it listens to Muzak over the intercom. It won't say if it loves me or the bittersweet aphasia of my body. "Your soul is as flat as a playing card," it says. I still haven't described it and it might die if I don't give it proper polish. "Open and say *ahh*. As in comma." Unless it prefers a dash to plug the hole.

But it has no penny, no slot. Why should it? Though it shines like copper—or something else that shines. Or once did. Now, I've cut it out of the story completely. Slash, slash. I had to make room (really nothing more than an uncluttered space) for the revision, maybe a flashback. The scene where I discover it once hid under my tongue! As if placed there by a child hiding the coin of his shame.

SATIE'S INSTRUCTIONS
FOR YOUR LOVE LIFE

With astonishment
Plug the O
of his mouth
with two fingers.
Talk dirty.

Light as an egg
Trace the curve of his wrist as he sleeps,
feel for the fault-
line.

Like a nightingale with a toothache
At the very moment it loosens,
swallow it
before it flies away.

Open your head
There is a switch
you must throw
to know death.

Here comes the lantern
Swing, swing it.
Thrust forward, stick it
out. Breathe through
the nose so you can
sing into every mouth,
light every orifice.

Muffle the sound
The pillow, the tears,
the torn bits, and stains—
these remains.

Dry as a cuckoo
Never stop
calling his name.
Even when he says
he'll leave
if you don't stop
calling his name.
Calmly stroll
from room to room
naming the dusty cushions
and pillows and the credenza,
using only his pet names.

Play on faded velvet
The percussive perspicacity
of the body beating inside its hairy
nudity is beauty in virtuosity.

Work it out yourself
It's you that plays the prop.
Work yourself out of it.
Leave the bed damp.

NIETZCHE, PASOLINI & I

"Why am I a destiny?"
—Friedrich Nietzsche

I know so little of myself,
even less of them,
so I'm stunned
when, in a dream,
on my knees,
I taunt Nietzsche,
calling him "the little minister."

He doesn't want to play,
holds his temples in his hands
like his head is Faberge,
or a soul, not that I know
anything of souls.

On all fours, I can only cry out
a long, ragged neigh, stomping
and violently flinging
back my head, a horse
whipped into terror,
front knees buckling
like prayer, steam rising
from my wounds.

I know so little of my desire,
but I feel lust for Pasolini,
who's been muttering,
"All sex is ironic."
He's wearing a black cravat
tied so tight his face is red.
When he tries to loosen it,
he gets erect, and cries some more.

It's all too much
for Nietzsche and I.
We embrace in a long kiss
that seems to answer
every question we've ever had.

Pasolini applauds.

LOVE POEM
TO CARL LINNAEUS

Would you bring me to Sweden,
like the rhubarb—sticky, sweet
rhubarb—you somehow grew there?
Sing to me the litany of other delights
you hoped would take hold
in your frigid Nordic homeland?
Tea plants, coffee beans,
ginger and coconut, silk worms,
cotton and clams!

Write across my body syllables
of fauna and flora, a patina of Latin
taxonomy etched onto my back.
Each *-us*, *-it*, and *-ate*
makes me stiff as the ivory bill
of the *Campephilus principalis*.
Hard as *Rhinoceros unicornis*
and *Rhinoceros sondaicus*.
Let's do it like *lepus californicus*,
bay at the scarlet moon like *canis lupus*,
and eat our luxurious binomials.

ALMOST A BEDROOM

PEAR, APPLE, PEACH

La poire, la pomme, la peche,
he sings as he shaves away
the sugar mountained past the rim
of the tin measuring cup—a sweep
that turns into an upturned palm.

The syrup of a pitted memory
swells from my stomach,
punches me back from the table,
where I break my nights
into a mire of sticky rinds,
bouquets of stiff baguettes—
pleas that share me with him.

I am secretly learning
the fruits as days.

He places a sugar cube—
soaked in his morning's coffee—
on my tongue (a shaking bone
clicking terribly, a scold
that scalds the soft,
peachy flesh of my mouth).

The days pass as I
count my teeth:
Lundi, Mardi, Mecredi.

AUBADE WITH PLUM

The waves crashing woke you, and you untangled our bodies.
Your limbs, taut and sundark, mine feeble and china-white,
   had somehow grown together in the night like the dune's pillow weeds.

Your shock at being there, the golden feathers of your bangs
brushing against my lips, was a coughed 'What the fuck.'

  I wish I had laughed

   when your canoe-shaped feet caught in the sandy, wrinkled sheets
and you swore again, nearly toppling (so clumsy!) as you slipped on

  the still-damp swimsuit, sounding like a zipper zipped down.
So this was how it began, how it ended: you scribbling a note—'Gone
   to Mickey D's for a coffee, some grub,' stopping for a moment

  (I held my breath)

   to stare at a gray seagull, cawing out to some small thing
drowning in the Atlantic shoals. And as you locked the door and left,
   I held what felt like a whole plum caught in my throat,

  and watched the sky turn from shades of plum
to goddam shades of plum.

WAITING ROOM

In the midst of anticipation
of the doctor's press on my bare chest,
his breath, the hairs on his chin, him
inches from the inside of my mouth—
an ordinary woman sits, the hem
of her pant leg rising to expose her ankle.
Nothing more. I am hypnotized,

in love the moment she nudges the cuff
of her black slacks up to her calf,
her hand digging into an itch
like a man's hand scratching his crotch
when no one's watching. How... *unlikely*
this is, from a boy who slakes
himself with thoughts of a long hair
tickling the base of a man's thick wrist,
that hand cupping my chin and guiding
my face down to his open fly.

I know there are dips in the human skin,
hollowed out like open mouths, places
meant to be found in the dark, fumbling
to fill or to excavate. I know the body
is a *volcano, / black, and full of ashes...*
/ spilling over / in rivulets of fire.

But her ankle—dangling like death,
the bone's horrifying knob, the moth-wing
skin sloping naked into her sandals.
I'm hard now. From nowhere
I am reaching down into her long body,

from mouth to vacant belly with its thin
tethers, soft buds of interior skin. I can't
breathe inside her awful underwater
so I push for the surface—a man's push,
emptying what it wants to fill.

ALMOST A BEDROOM

1

The sickly sweet smell
of bread-still-baking
wafting from the end
of the bed, a yeast
your feet put off.

2

The tremble of your voice,
singing over and over the same
measure of a madrigal of kissings
(the song that won you States
in high school, the scare-
crow with golden pipes).

I feel the notes inside me
as we prune in the bath,
hoping that if I remain still—
no ripples, no breath—
you'll move on, finally
accept we lost the harmony.

3

The peel of skin
from your blooming pec...

a tattoo of the phoenix
burns gold, purple

before disappearing
under my tiny hands

in milky swirls of
cool, cool oatmeal lotion

4

The taste of your breath
after too much wine
and your skin, still asleep,
steeped in the humid fog
of a summer drowse...

The imagined taste of honey
as a bumblebee lands on the red
rim of the empty wine glass
set daringly on the nightstand's edge...

5

The fine blond hair
I twist between my fingers,
the damp feeling
of your wet face
against my shoulder
after you tell me about him,
and plead for me to stay.

COLD COMFORT

There is comfort
in sleeping among your shoes
on the floor beside our bed
those nights you are away.

There is comfort
in wrestling away a blanket, naked,
cool on the bare floor, relieved
of the ceiling's dark eyes.

There is comfort
on the nights you curl, uncurl
and twist beside me, dancing
through my fever dream.

There is comfort
far away from us, too, isn't there.
A neatly tucked-in bed, a single
pair of shoes left at the door.

STILL LIFE WITH JARS

You gone, I dream of the clay jars again—
in rows, most filled with a hand's cup of rain.

Into one I tip out apple slices
from my palm, all pulpy moons, pieces

to tell our fortune by the points' direction.
East means "work of art"; the composition

fulfills the loss of self or sleep or shame.
South means for me to steal my way

along the baseboards, up the walls, insect-
step around the jar's rim, the risk of sex,

too, like the risk of falling to the water.
North's rule: I must learn how to shatter

the jars you keep empty, a sky so black
you'll not learn to paint it. The canvas cracks

with thick acrylic swamps of tangled lines,
your plan to shadow what you cannot find.

West: your love of objects without souls, lives
without life or substance. Yet you still lie,

lie still on top of me in bed, drawing
in your head other jars, all sweating,

filled by the weight of holding stones,
smooth, water-worried—nothing like the bone

you tap beneath my bed the night it rains,
your empty easel in the yard, the names

of all your still lifes keeping me asleep,
the recitation of your work, how sweet

clay tastes, how cool water from a jar,
how real a dream can be, the danger

of holding apples to the moon,
pouring water out of jars for you.

BLOOD IN THE CUM

1

When he makes love,
he imagines himself
wrapping delicate packets
of precious white tea
in crisp squares of pink tissue.

2

He hides under the swirling
chest hairs I kiss what he says
are spider bites from our lovemaking.
They spread and mottle
like a web of broken capillaries.

3

A poet, he cheats at the game
of diagnosis: a love poem
is his way to sew
our two mouths shut
with a kiss so thin it's invisible.

4

He writes, *Blood in the cum*
is the scarlet ribbon
in an egg's albumen,
a mistake of embryonic petals
coiled at its center.

FINDING AN EGG IN WINTER

Plucked
from the snow
you are moon
cold.

The shell of you
is rough with bumps
like taste buds.

Under your surface
a hairline
is whining
its way
to a crack.

I tuck you
in the warm
pocket
of my thick
wool coat.

Please…
stay put
as I foot
about the city
looking for
oh, who
knows!
a first love
or proof
of alien life.

Until then,
please
do not break.
I would lose
what little
I've left.

A MAN STANDING

The news reports *a mass stranding*,
the deadliest in over 100 years—
thousands of dying 'flying squid'
still thrumming, seizing amidst
a tantalizingly salty oxygen,
their bodies leaving grooves
in the sand at La Jolla Cove, proof
their tentacles reached back for the sea.

12 tons of dead and dying squid,
a mass stranding. Yet at first
I heard: *A man standing*,
and saw a man on earth
freshly turned, his hands
held palms out, facing the sky
in supplication, a gesture modernity
has made ironic—

They have humanlike eyeballs. They made
these strange noises as they were dying.
Some the size of human 2-year olds
tumbled by the surf and washed ashore
while chasing a school of grunion,
a fish that spawns on the sand at high tide.
Dosidicus gigas *normally nestle*
in the eastern Pacific Ocean.

It's the word *nestle*
that calls up an image of us
lovingly tucked into our graves.
We line up, fold our hands
in resignation, and lie down
in plots neatly edged
by chalky copses of dwarf birch.
Their limbs reach for the wind,
sheltering bodies stranded
in the memory of the dying day,
an ocean; we drift on our backs
in calm waters—even love
wasn't enough to reach back for.

SICK ROOM

My love, my Lethe (an ebb has begun),
  the terror of being alone
  is replaced by my fingers' arthritic
  worrying of your braided bones
  to ease the caving ribs away.

Fever is hostage for you,
  my dear wound, my truce.

My spit is a tasteless poultice
  and my breath is
  leaves of mint on your chest.

I am ridden, I
  am prone, here.
  I am the ever-present room,
  curtaining contagion.

An original, iron heat
  snakes through you,
  and I can only press it deeper—invisible
  waves—into the scored creases
  I've left.

Cold press, a cloth,
  an orphaned promise:
  If I sleep, if I leave
  you, I will vanish
  like the pearled ice here,
  already brittle in their bowl.

EPITHALAMION

Still dark when you leave our new bed,
you find me here at the stove.
You kiss my neck *good morning*
and lay your head on my back
to hear me breathe.

For now I am indebted to these eggs,
the union of their sly balance
with my want of shape and symmetry.

My hand curls around another egg,
and I imagine an unbreakable sound.
My tongue is curved to meet it, feeling
the pull and urge of the pre-lingual.

I try the long vowels, drawing
my voice into wide ribbons
as I crack the egg on the bowl's rim.

Like a natural magic your arms appear
circling my waist; with your chin on my neck
you ask if I slept well. I say you need to shave.
You rub stubble into my skin.

I watch your body bend toward
coming daylight as you set wildflowers
in my grandmother's cobalt blue milk-pitcher,
open the window, push apart the curtains.

Morning sun hums from the homemade vase.
If there is an unbreakable sound,
it's this soft burn, not like a vowel,
but like a touch, unnamable.

NOTES

CHRISTOPHER LOOKS is a collage using the Google results from a search of the term "[The poet's first name] looks like..."

ROSALINE
Italicized lines from William Shakespeare's *Romeo and Juliet*.

THIEF
In 1995, an Incan girl was found preserved in ice on a mountaintop near Arequipa, Peru. Archeologists named her Juanita the Ice Maiden.

"I HAND YOU LIKE AN ORANGE TO A CHILD." A collage of final words. Key to quotations:

Title: Edgar Lee Masters

I
1. J.M. Barrie
2. Olavo Bilac [Brazilian poet]
3. Goethe: "More light"
4-5. O. Henry
6. Warren G. Harding [asking his wife to read flattering newspaper accounts of him]
7-8. Sadako Sasaki [12-year-old Hiroshima atomic bomb victim, tasting tea before dying in her sleep]

II
1. Emily Dickinson [in a letter to Louise and Frances Norcross, May 1886]
2. Emily Dickinson
3. Victor Hugo
4. Frédéric Chopin
5-6. Jessica Dubroff [Seven-year-old who had been encouraged by her parents to set a record as the youngest person to fly across the United States. Her plane plummeted to earth]
7. Jean Cocteau [referring to his own death]
8. Gustavo Adolfo Bécquer [Spanish poet]
9. Victor Hugo
9. John Quincy Adams

III
1, 3. Marie Antoinette: "Pardon me, sir." [to her executioner, after accidentally stepping on his toes]
2, 4-6. Yukio Mishima [After shouting "Long live His Imperial

Majesty!" in order to encourage a coup to return the Emperor to power, he performed ritual suicide]
7. Isadora Duncan: "Goodbye my friends. I go in glory!"

IV
1. Freud: "This is absurd!"
1-2. Amelia Earhart
3, 5. Hegel
4. Archimedes: "Don't disturb my circles!" [to a Roman soldier who was bothering him as he worked equations in the sand]

V
1-3. Akiva ben Joseph [ca.50-ca.135, burned at the stake, along with his Torah]
4-5. John Huss [Czech reformer priest who was burned at the stake]
6. David Hume [famed atheist]

SATIE'S INSTRUCTIONS FOR YOUR LOVE LIFE: Erik Satie (1866-1925) was an eccentric Impressionist French composer and musician known for using unconventional musical instructions in his scores. The italicized portions are actual examples of these notations.

ALMOST A BEDROOM: This phrase is taken from Jack Spicer's "A Birthday Poem for Jim (and James) Alexander," in *My Vocabulary Did This To Me: The Collected Poetry of Jack Spicer* (Wesleyan University Press, 2008). In the book's introduction, the editors Peter Gizzi and Kevin Killian note that Spicer "felt that if he could just write well enough, the poem would become 'almost a bedroom.'"

WAITING ROOM: Italicized lines are from Elizabeth Bishop's poem "In the Waiting Room."

A MAN STANDING: Italicized portions originated from an *Associated Press* article, dated 7/27/02.

ABOUT THE POET

Christopher Hennessy is the author of *Outside the Lines: Talking with Contemporary Gay Poets* (University of Michigan Press). He earned an MFA from Emerson College and currently is a Ph.D. candidate in English Literature at the University of Massachusetts-Amherst. He was included in *Ploughshares'* special "Emerging Writers" edition, and his poetry, interviews, and book reviews have appeared in *American Poetry Review*, *Verse*, *Cimarron Review*, *The Writer's Chronicle*, *The Bloomsbury Review*, *Court Green*, *OCHO*, *Crab Orchard Review*, *Natural Bridge*, *Wisconsin Review*, *Brooklyn Review*, *Memorious*, and elsewhere. His poems have appeared or are forthcoming in anthologies of gay poets, persona poetry, and poets of social justice. His prose is also included in *DIVAS: Gay Men on the Women Who Shaped Their Lives* (University Wisconsin Press). Hennessy is a longtime associate editor for *The Gay & Lesbian Review-Worldwide*.